See them dance naked

    watching starry midnight skies

        tiptoeing with care

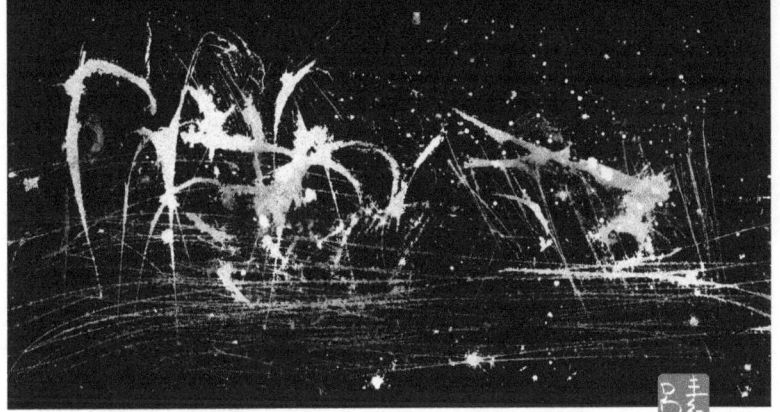

The Big Little Book of Thoughts

Growth, Love, Nurture, Aspire, Wisdom

KARRIE ROSS

The BIG Little Book of Thoughts
Growth, Love, Nurture, Aspire, Wisdom
Karrie Ross

All rights reserved
Copyright ©1998-2012 Be It Now! Karrie Ross
A Be-It-Now! Book

All rights reserved. No part of this book may be reproduced or
transmitted in any form or by any means, electronic or mechanical,
including photocopying, recording or by any other information storage and retrieval system, without written permission from the author,
except for the inclusion of brief quotations in a review. Be It Now! is
a registered trademark and copyrighted property of Be It Now!.

Printed in the United States of America

Book design: www.KarrieRoss.com
Illustrations: Karrie Ross 2011

Books are available for special promotions and premiums.
For details contact:

Published by Be It Now!® Books
Los Angeles, CA 90066
info@beitnow.com   www.TheLifeDialogue.com

ISBN 13: 978-09723366-1-1

*Give yourself
the gift of inspiration.
The thoughts contained
in this book are from my never
ending journey of self discovery...
I hope you'll
use them to encourage the
discovery of your own adventure,
consider them as a stimulation
to get you paying attention.*

Growth

Here we sit within
    searching for the mountain top
      yet see only clouds

    Water moved by air
  becomes rain in times of need
        but what of the wind

Growth, Love, Nurture, Aspire, Wisdom

Today I will be conscious of my actions showing compassion to all.

Another sees gray
>become skies when its raining
>>I see sweet stillness

>Allow others
>to journey with you and the
>stream widens towards the end
>with smiles

>When fire catches
feel magic flames dancing
>>over rock gardens

Growth, Love, Nurture, Aspire, Wisdom

When dreams fade away the jewels
they leave take in your hand and
scatter to the wind onto different
journeys each will bring full of
wonder adventure and stories to tell
for insights abundant discovery
exposed each experience in
perspective to the eyes seeing
encourage your feelings to sore beyond
ever imagined shores and from the
clouds looking down
become once more the more.

Can you see it the energy of the ages moving
        through your systems
    bringing you to a place of presence in the now
        ever wonder how you got here
dancing skies with only the stars to lead your way
    joining hands with humanity creating passions
        growing in strength and perseverance
            through times past
        memories glancing in mirrors to what was
            never more to be alone in the brush
        as the new landscape is painted in
            perfect tones its strokes
featuring reds and blues on fields
    of white flowers
            ever growing
                being free.

Growth, Love, Nurture, Aspire, Wisdom

All starts within,
the connection to
ourselves…from there,
others will
join the journey.

When you put passion in the doing, you create a state of being.

Stand tall in your choices, allow for change and go with it.

Resistance is inreaction. When you include resistance in your healing, your seeing and your pain... negativity is stopped.

Growth, Love, Nurture, Aspire, Wisdom

By making choices
you em-power
those choices
to fill the energy
with possibility.

Be in the moment.
Experience
your
surroundings
with
consideration,
observation
and ease.

Growth, Love, Nurture, Aspire, Wisdom

We only
know,
become
aware,
by
experiences.

Within the wonders of intention, our life appears.

The state of no reaction.

A possible jumping off space?

The power is
in the doing

being

silent patience.

Choose wisely
the mirror you
look in –

growth is always
an option.

Just what is making a difference?

Why not just be one!

Growth, Love, Nurture, Aspire, Wisdom

If things aren't the way you want them to be? Look into yourself for the strength to continue and change.

Don't expect others to do it for you!

Each time you
feel like quitting,
turn those feelings
around into
the next
beginning...
use the energy
wisely.

Judgements lead nowhere. Compliments open doors.

Watch and learn –
then do and be.

Growth, Love, Nurture, Aspire, Wisdom

How many times
can we start over –
let me see –
moment by moment!

Gee, that's a lot!!!

Take a stand
for what you want.
Welcome change
no matter what
the outcome.

Growth, Love, Nurture, Aspire, Wisdom

Good, bad,
right, wrong,
eh! words.
Their meaning
is what
YOU make it!

Still your thoughts.
Goodness,
let the
sanity begin!

So many things,
thoughts, stop us.

Why give such
power to negativity?

So something happened…
why not make
it mean
something good.

Growth, Love, Nurture, Aspire, Wisdom

Life is an experience. Don't miss it... Live NOW!

Once awakened
there is no return
to sleep.

Be brave.
See reality
everywhere.

Possibilities are endless.
Create time now
as each moment passes,
don't miss a beat of
your life.

Observing and questioning growth seems a never ending journey to light.

Growth, Love, Nurture, Aspire, Wisdom

Excite the dawn
each day, explore
the road less
traveled, creating
situations that
encourage growth –
be special to yourself,
taste your passions fully.

Love freedom,
sense security,
have the courage
to test the unknown
and begin life.

Within our unconsciousness there lies an individual waiting for us to awaken!

Within my space,
I have a life,
Within my life,
I have the time,
Within the time,
I have thoughts,
Within my thoughts,
I AM.

Awareness of the
soul is the
knowledge of the self.

Self-knowledge is the
essence of life. Creation
rests within us…
the contemplative soul.

When everything is
said and done.

Life continues
and goes on.

Growth, Love, Nurture, Aspire, Wisdom

Be the
good-humor
of your life.

The seven faces
of life:
Up.
Down.
Left.
Right.
Forward.
Backward.
NOW!

Growth, Love, Nurture, Aspire, Wisdom

You must know where
you've been
to go forward…
omit the strife.

Take time to be
with nature,
welcome it's
blessings.

Growth, Love, Nurture, Aspire, Wisdom

Increase the speed with which you perceive.

Stimulate your eccentricity.

You must know
where you've been
to go forward…
omit the strife.

Growth, Love, Nurture, Aspire, Wisdom

Feeling blocked? Examine your attachments and fixations.

Clean.

Make sure to
remember
yourself…

as you leave
the house!

Growth, Love, Nurture, Aspire, Wisdom

To wish a
conscious wish.
To be present
in the voicing.
Is the most
powerful action
in the world.

Try not to think about what you think you will loose.

Turn your perspective to what is gained.

Growth, Love, Nurture, Aspire, Wisdom

There is no wrong connection.

Without change nothing moves forward. And if it's not the forward you thought it would be, consider this …
it's in a state of becoming.

What does your
internal dialogue
sound like?
If it's not working for
your progress and
growth…
then reconsider
and change it.
Talk into your goals.

Expand and contract.
Always moving
and changing.
The act of becoming is
never ending.

Growth, Love, Nurture, Aspire, Wisdom

Simple is the journey once unfolded...

the origami of life!

Intend the direction you want.
Each step you take towards it brings energy to it, creating a constant state of becoming.

Growth, Love, Nurture, Aspire, Wisdom

Watch what you do when you do it, acknowledge your abilities.

When we live
too long in
personality…
we loose sight
of life.

Growth, Love, Nurture, Aspire, Wisdom

It's not so much how
I see you,
as how you see
I see you.

Peace is when
the length
of your vision
can be held.

You only have
control over how
you are being,
not how
others perceive
you.

Wispy wandering
free now the reeds bend with wind
sweetly passing time

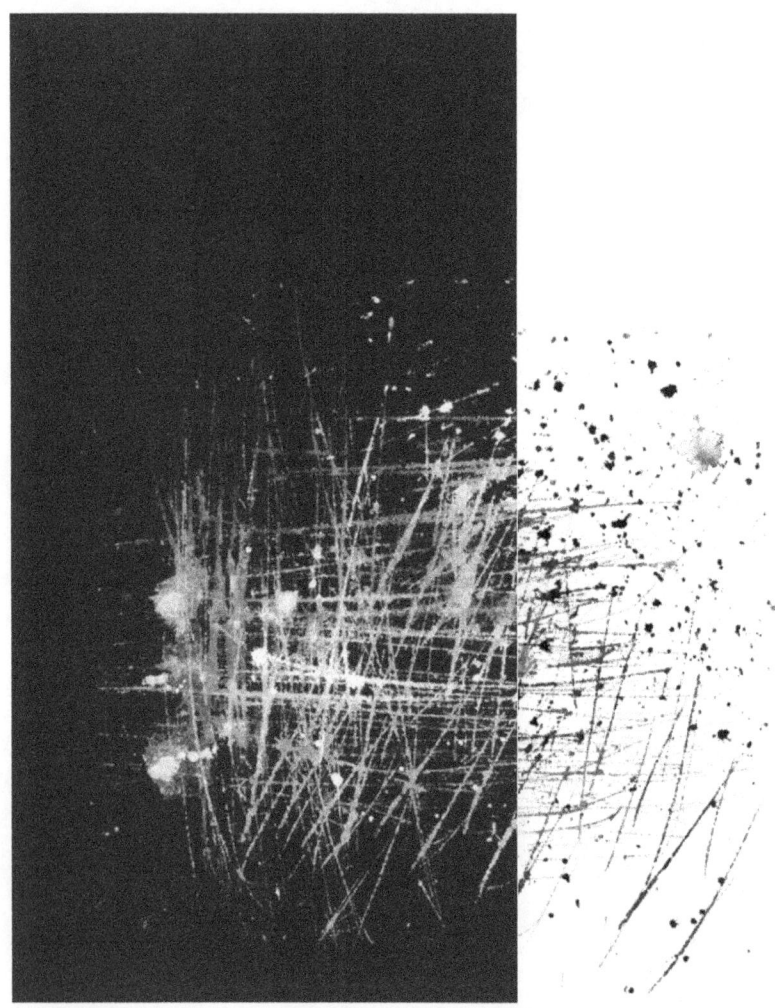

Growth, Love, Nurture, Aspire, Wisdom

Love

Mystery you say what is there for you
a shoe and a lizard with something to hoot whoa
stop the owl turn over the bowl something is hiding
only the big toe knows and the yellow light in the
distance does sound a thunder of cheers for the clue
that is found woopie shock us again and again and
again bring us the movement we'll search to the end
change is our purpose our goal and our friend purple
rests at the end of a pin and the spider comes in
from the cold to heat up the den welcoming flies and
bugs from the winter's shimmering glow of the story
of life and well it is told when the butterfly rests on
the little girl's bed sending wonder adventure straight
to her head the hair there is pulled releasing the
tension allowing the white dove to sing in the
procession into the depths of the night and the dawn
they all come the dragons and cranes their work very
well done spreading a cover of red that softens the
snow as a footprint marking time to the dance and
the green grass sways to and fro swish swish of the
waves ring a sweet smell of life as we live it peek-a-
boo I See You...

Dancing with emotions.

It is not the nature of the human condition to be able to handle the full experience of all feelings at once.
I've found the tendency is to take it gradually, limited exposure over time until we finally are able to fully taste the emotion to move with/from it completely and with some space of comfort…it becomes a learned experience, like dancing as we assimilate it into our lives.

Fairies dance the moon
arising over the garden lovely
delightfully delicious pastries
baked fresh each morning
opening with insights from the
night before when little dew
drops fell upon the bed
leaves rolling in the breeze
into the sun shining bright and
clear the shimmer of the shy whose
story is told as the clouds pass.

Growth, Love, Nurture, Aspire, Wisdom

Today I will share
my joy of life,
infusing wonder
and delight.

Create the ability to be passionate. Develop the 'muscle' of feelings. Be alowing of them. Welcome them into your being.

Growth, Love, Nurture, Aspire, Wisdom

Exercise your
ability to feel…
deeply
fully
entirely
expressively

Wellness of the mind, no thoughts confined… physical movement brings healing.

Leave your thoughts open to others, allow their love to attend.

Turn your perspective to 'having' in life…
joy and love.
When you allow only the feeling of loss,
you are empty at best!

Growth, Love, Nurture, Aspire, Wisdom

Have you ever watched flowers as they sit in a vase, their stems entwined at the base, their blooms flare apart at the top, flying free knowing support and being loved?

Courage is of
the heart.

Of love
expressed.

There is no 'alone' when I open to life. Only mystery,
wonder, adventure, delight…

What is the thread the focus, that runs through your life?

Create it.
Be it's passion.

Things die when
we stop sharing.

Develop yourself as a
possibility.

Don't loose the magic!

(reframed is said like this)

Hold tight to the magic!

Growth, Love, Nurture, Aspire, Wisdom

Be the cause of
what's to be.
Be expression.
Be risk.
Be in the heart of
all being.

The flowers that bloom in the heart, bring wonders and magical delight!

Growth, Love, Nurture, Aspire, Wisdom

Within each breath comes the magic of life. Lets boogie!

Be light my soul
and welcome the
meaning of love…
hug a tree
kiss a frog!

Growth, Love, Nurture, Aspire, Wisdom

Freedom comes in
many forms –
let's make life
one big splatter
of Joy!

When we choose from
the heart –
the rest of the body
follows.

Growth, Love, Nurture, Aspire, Wisdom

Take a chance on
yourself –
life is made from
experiences.

Emotions
are like a
bucking bronco.
You gotta keep
trying them
to build trust.

Growth, Love, Nurture, Aspire, Wisdom

Feel the tension.
Follow it's energy.
Release the hold.
Get on with life.

Fun. Play. Explore.
See the mind alive
in creativity.

Smile and laugh the
wrinkles away!

Give of yourself
each day.
Smile.
You won't believe
the response.

Simple. Complex.
How will I be today?
What
are my
possibilities
to play?

Growth, Love, Nurture, Aspire, Wisdom

The elegance
of love.
Dance.
Spaces creates
movement.

Meet each day
with an open heart,
truth
and sincerity.

Be true to the
movement of life.
Fully feel what is
going on, bring
it into your space.
Eat of it.

Bring whimsey
and delight
to all you do.
Be still.
Be now.
Be you.

No matter
who you are,
be real,
be true,
bring love
to all you touch.

Where-in the flowers grow, love blooms abundantly.

Be mischievous.
Be alive.
Be sensual.
Be serious.
Be yourself.
Be seen.
Motivate others.
Participate in life.

Strive for the higher,
the better,
feel the passion
of life.

Growth, Love, Nurture, Aspire, Wisdom

Meet the world
with an open heart.
Gather the goodness
towards you.

It is from within
that we must look
for the acceptance
of truth.
All comes from
inside us.
Perceptions.

Growth, Love, Nurture, Aspire, Wisdom

Become the
fly-in-the-corner,
take a look at
who you are being…
know that
to live
is to change.

Freedom is something you make for your self.

Acceptance of the responsibility of commitment of the involvement to yourself and others. Wow! what a concept!

For all the years
I've not been there.
For all the years
to come.
Passion in my giving.
Joy becomes me.

Growth, Love, Nurture, Aspire, Wisdom

Reach out for freedom.
Reach out for truth.
Join hands
in peace and
togetherness.

Life is energy.
Don't waste it!

Unity.
Dance to the magic.
Thrill to the touch
of another.
Create the poetry
of life.

Give yourself of yourself…live the secret of happiness.

The fall of my life, the rains came —
deep howling of the soul — then clipped as a dead rose to allow the joy exposed.

Love.
To look into the
eyes of another
and know fully why you
are loved.
To see yourself reflected
in them, renewed,
refreshed daily.

Growth, Love, Nurture, Aspire, Wisdom

The gift of giving… the magic of enchantment.

Beyond
there is another reality
some won't ever see,
full of whimsy, wonder
and free...
the now.

The gift of giving goes beyond the obvious.

Sometimes all it takes is a smile.

Love is a gift.
It's about 'having'
the experience.

The have in love is the
experience.

Growth, Love, Nurture, Aspire, Wisdom

Joyful dance
into the night,
share with me
your beauty.

Touch the ground lightly.

Growth, Love, Nurture, Aspire, Wisdom

Live.
Love.
Laugh.

Sometimes
we need to follow
to learn to lead.

Growth, Love, Nurture, Aspire, Wisdom

Step into life.
Watch with me,
smiles so sweet
they touch our souls
with love sublime,
eternally.

When you make a
commitment the
universe hears you
and assists...
follow your passions
with delight, wonder
and risk!

Growth, Love, Nurture, Aspire, Wisdom

Find your light, and faith befriends your journey.

Where sun meets water
    at 2 in the afternoon
        sandcrabs hide in waves

    6" whitewall tires
        make a difference if driving
        58 EDSEL

Spiders create webs
    when dew covers them gently
    diamonds come to life

        Walking through forests
    see each tree absorb sunshine
        touch their leaves gently

Growth, Love, Nurture, Aspire, Wisdom

Nurture

A distance walked once
        seems far easier the next
                moved perspective

      Dreams form ways of thought
             when spoken from the heart
                    encourage others

Wind chimes create sound
        when silent ponder openly
the next hurricane

      Mysteries when shared
            doors showing different knobs
                beauty in each one

Today I will honor myself and others, encouraging balance and expansion.

The Big Little Book of Thoughts

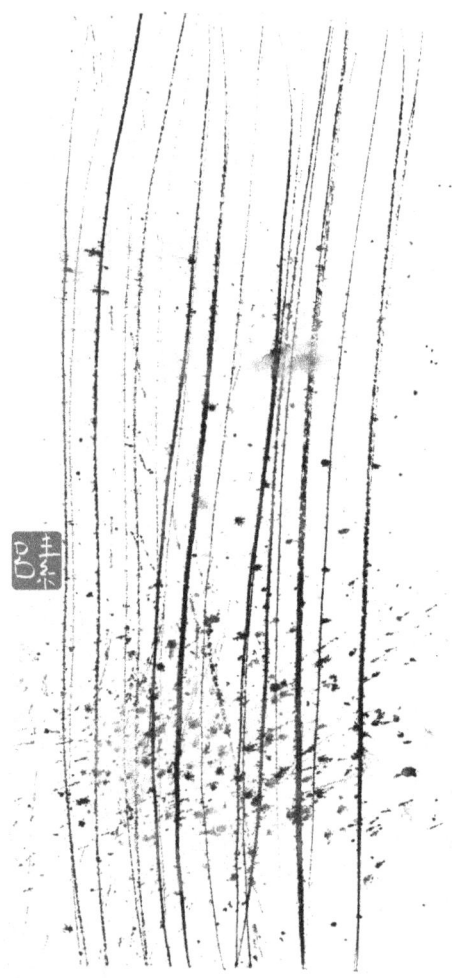

Bamboo measures space
   joints indicate each section
     circling time with hugs

We create our world.
Find others who think like you do. Converse with them sharing your thoughts and feelings. Surround yourself with the things you love, allow them to nourish you and give to you all that makes your life full and self expressive.

Strength of purpose, purity of actions. Build the base that feeds life.

Growth, Love, Nurture, Aspire, Wisdom

Strive for balance within your structure, as you be, so will they honor.

Clarity is a decision. Something happens and a choice appears. Eliminate misery, find the power of decision. Be clear with purpose and direction.

What's so.
Just let it go.
Drop it.
Nothing is wrong.
Live into it.

When outside meets inside,
a duality speaks one thought.
Clarity of death the cycle
begins. Blessing achievements,
challenging perceptions,
risking. A meeting
of two minds
experiencing new thought.
A state of grace, when all
speaks as one.

Growth, Love, Nurture, Aspire, Wisdom

Decisions
Choices
Open your eyes
to the power of
intention.

There is only comfort and discomfort.

Growth, Love, Nurture, Aspire, Wisdom

Learn the voice from within and doors will open.

Establish a position to take.
Then project your being from that point of view.

Ask anything… there is only acceptance or decline… be unreasonable.

Accomplishment lives in the moment you voice it and evolves into fulfillment of its being.

Speak of possibilities. Invite another to take action.

Be responsible
for who
you are being
with others.

Seek external adventures to stimulate the internal experience…
be curious, know you are being taken care of.

When 'it's' real
you feel 'it'
deeply
'it' resonates
within
creating a vibration.

Growth, Love, Nurture, Aspire, Wisdom

When you know you can stop…

there is nowhere you can't go!

Why are you acting that
way if 'it'
no longer makes
a difference?

Growth, Love, Nurture, Aspire, Wisdom

Creation
is within us,
the contemplative soul.

Share of yourself –
create communion
with life.

Growth, Love, Nurture, Aspire, Wisdom

The power of intention when acted upon, fills the soul with the energy of life.

Decisions bring choices which
produce clarity.
Create a non-static world.

Growth, Love, Nurture, Aspire, Wisdom

Youth is a state of mind... so is life!

Why create disharmony – you know what I mean… gossip, complaints, judgements – what is that all about anyways!

With each day open to
the continuous beauty
that comes your way –
for it is the energy
of life and new
beginnings.

Remember you are in control of your attitude – listen for the sound of truth within yourself and others.

Blah, Blah, Blah, the continuous negative chatter we create in our mind that keeps us from our destiny... Laugh at it's demands!

Even the smallest
of intentions,
makes a
difference.

Be clear with your purpose and direction. Find the power of decision. Stick-to-it-ness.

The sun is up.
The moon's asleep.
Twinkle Twinkle
little feet.
Looks to me the
birds will sing
of games to play and
dreams to meet.
Open to life's
blessings.

Dance the dance.
Be free.
Open your eyes
and see.
The beauty
in all that is.

Expect nothing.
Accept everything.
Relax. The journey
is never ending.
You choose the
direction.

Allow what has
'happened' to take
it's place in your life.
Assimilate and
continue.

The time to think seems
a luxury to some.
Acceptance of the
unknown cannot
be thought out…
just understood
as necessary.

Growth, Love, Nurture, Aspire, Wisdom

What an awesome power it is to be ourselves. Authenticity of being.

For every step in life we take… another one awaits!

At times we say
good-bye to parts of
our lives. Whatever they
may be. So evasive with
their going, not sure they'd
ever been. Then there is
the cheery hello to the rest
of what is…

Be more at peace with
how you are –
a small mind will not
take you far.

Growth, Love, Nurture, Aspire, Wisdom

You know
you're there
by the look
on their face(s),

Ponder and be attentive to the knowledge your body shares. The activity of emotions.

Growth, Love, Nurture, Aspire, Wisdom

Is there a choiceless awareness?

Be your thoughts.
be positive,
be truth,
be beauty,
be love.
be now.

Growth, Love, Nurture, Aspire, Wisdom

Life is full of rude
awakenings…
have you looked lately?
Don't be so quick
to judge another.

State the obvious.
See it, feel it,
participate in it.
Space/time/light.

Growth, Love, Nurture, Aspire, Wisdom

Movements increase.
The dancing explodes.
Bring balance to
the energy.
Transition unfolds.

We all make our own
way in the world.
Ask,
watch and listen
you will be shown.

Growth, Love, Nurture, Aspire, Wisdom

Find home.

Within.

When two
bubbles unite
they disappear
into one bloom.

Creating support promotes the feeling of strength within the friendship.

Mysterious
Magical
Miraculous
Marvelous
Mind
Maneuvers

Growth, Love, Nurture, Aspire, Wisdom

Fulfill your
dreams
within each
moment
as it occurs.

When you
teach
what you learn,
it becomes more
of you.

Growth, Love, Nurture, Aspire, Wisdom

Courage.

Persistence and determination...are the building blocks
of dreams!

Growth, Love, Nurture, Aspire, Wisdom

Aspire

where is the butterfly?
how fast it is
we don't even see it go
yet there it is
again

then there is the ordinary garden spider
spinning a web in the middle of the yard with no
obvious attachments
magically appears bringing wonder
why is not to be asked
it just is

and the winter's golden sun
beaming through my window
brings a calm to my being
the heater turns on
to smell up the house with the
burning off of the summer's silence
joyous in its rebirth
and now

Growth, Love, Nurture, Aspire, Wisdom

Today I will be receptive of what is and welcome the day and it's blessings.

Not knowing vibrates
deep inside as silence moves free
opening with fear

* * *

Spring green grass growing
lusciously covers the ground
wash before you eat

* * *

Day's journey may end
in darkness by afternoon
wait, don't shut your eyes

* * *

Freedom joyously
catching out-spread wings moving
flying fresh smooth alive

* * *

Spiraling new stars
meet bursting with energy
plug into their WOW!

* * *

Sounds heard through brick walls
muffled like noisy old cars
penetrating peace

The day has passed and my life has moved
from one story to another each step of the
way people I meet welcome the freshness
their morning coffee brings to the donuts in
the pink box sitting on the counter is the
place to be on Mondays and everyone is
sharing time for experiencing weekends
different from the weekdays somewhere they
have separated days into sections keeping the
separation strong trying hard not to get lost in
the wilderness of choosing a different
perspective seeking their desires

Fearful is one
who once observes,
does not participate
and pass on the lessons.

Growth, Love, Nurture, Aspire, Wisdom

Fly with the dove,
bring creativity into
sight, welcome
it's gifts.

Create new patterns of thinking, doing, being. Be calm, smile, laugh, express, share.

Confidence begins when you commit to who you are being… live your vision.

Create something from nothing.

Lets get serious
you say? OK.
I'll play today, but
tomorrow let's change
the game.

Right here, right NOW
is being, the memory
lives on inside...gentle
softness in the night as
a light shinning bright
remember
it always.

Be unreasonable.
Be unstoppable.
Take the power to be
a difference.

What happens
is action and
no reaction equals
a miracle…breaking the
perceived reality.

What comes into our lives, is not yet written. Take your pen and write a book you can live into.

Growth, Love, Nurture, Aspire, Wisdom

Spiral into the continuous movement of change.

Live your life
forward into what's next.
Plan projects, create
results.

Feeling scarred
or worried?
Be concerned and
cautious. Change
the words you use and
your perspective
changes too!

What is your
focus in life?
Why complicate things,
it's easy.

When you allow another to control your choices, it's you who change, not them.

Just when you
think no one
is going to
tell you…
the words show up!

Growth, Love, Nurture, Aspire, Wisdom

Sometimes
we need to follow,
to learn,
to lead.

Some of us
need more control than
others…
or at least the
illusion of
it's being.

Sweetness and light, all is right, see the space for discovery.

I met a little man today, who told me not to worry. He said that things will slowly change, except for those in a hurry.

Growth, Love, Nurture, Aspire, Wisdom

Begin each day, take chances – disrupt your routine.

That which was
yesterday
is now
and tomorrow
until we see
and change.

Growth, Love, Nurture, Aspire, Wisdom

In the course of deciding have we forgotten what to ask?

Big and effective.
Small and simple.
The difference is
in your perception.

Growth, Love, Nurture, Aspire, Wisdom

It's all about imagination.

Holding on creates
a boundary to prevent
going further.

Growth, Love, Nurture, Aspire, Wisdom

Life is what we
make it…
be mindful
of what
you wish.

Beyond the now
is the
hereafter.

When the veils
of perception
are raised,
then we will
see things as they
really are.

Permanence
is the illusion.
Change is the reality.

We all fall back
a few steps
some of us are
just more allowing
about it.

Change
IS
power.

The future
is as set
as the past.
It's <u>our</u>
<u>point of view</u>
that changes.

The magic of
our soul
leads us,
befriends us knowing,
trusting,
believing.

Growth, Love, Nurture, Aspire, Wisdom

I love the rain…
with broad strokes
the canvas
is painted.

There is a limit
to what we will
put up with.
When it is reached,
the silliest, smallest thing
can break the spell…
truth reviled.
Choices to be made,
a life to create.

Growth, Love, Nurture, Aspire, Wisdom

How do we know
to dot our 'i's'
and cross our 't's'
when we are writing?
Watch the activity...observation.

Celebrate
the journey.
I am
what I've become.
Creation.

Growth, Love, Nurture, Aspire, Wisdom

When I've been there...
I bring it home,
the taste of
energy that
feeds my soul.

Dream your dance, create the flow of everlasting peace.

Simplicity of thought
and line.
Expressions.
Explore.
Experiences.

Share possibilities.
Be present.
Be generous.
Create life.

What is the story you've created? Turn your weaknesses into strengths. Create space where there isn't any!

Have conversations that move, stimulate, make a difference.

Growth, Love, Nurture, Aspire, Wisdom

"We" are more alike than we think!

Expand.

Look at yourself.
How are you being perceived?
Bring the vision home and expand.

Growth, Love, Nurture, Aspire, Wisdom

Share your focus.
Watch them come.

Things die when you stop sharing. Develop yourself as a possibility.

Intention brings tension which in turn creates action–Wow! what a rush!

Once you make
'it' an absolute
that's what it remains…
until then it's free
in the wind…
you choose.

What is it you
want to feel?
Consider your feelings
about the people,
things, etc.
around you.
Observe the ones
that aren't fitting
your dreams…
your vision of self.

The journey is long and full of trails. You'll be traveling many miles. But what you find, you can keep. Where you go, is where you seek. So open your eyes and you might see another part of eternity.

Growth, Love, Nurture, Aspire, Wisdom

Sometimes when light
comes into
our lives, fear blinds
our perception
so we can't see
it's beauty.

Create a state of harmony.
The difference is in how we see.

Growth, Love, Nurture, Aspire, Wisdom

Wisdom

Interesting how the way is shown in the cobblestones or seashells on the beach hanging out with the waves of sun light and sea-gulls flying into the wind tunnel as the test for astronauts go on each day from dawn until darkness falls over the horizon and the crickets chirp out the message that the eggs are already cooked if an X is marked on their shell sitting with the simple message of time in the fullness of the hour the power charges
the battery and the music plays notes bouncing on the doorstep down the walk into the street toward the corner kids playing hopscotch distanced from
cowboys and indians of days past as the train pulls from the station on its journey up the coast to the beer-boiled shrimp and bloody marys tea cakes and champaigne to toast a sun setting over the ocean with child on shoulders gently caressing the moment between words spoken in tones resembling drums of the nile pacing the barges movement testing the wind creating a never ending ripple into the lake on the shore the reeds sway and respond to the stimulation the touching caressing deep into the darkness of the water a soul reliving their kiss attending to details as mystery dissolves on fingertips dipped in honey a sweetness sure to bring the bees and butterfly's watching observing what the next moment will reveal.

Today I will acknowledge my fears, opening to creativity and participation.

Love in its freshness
        seems small to the human eye
                where is the butterfly

        Within the cocoon
    creating transformation
        off wiggles the worm

Touching the new leaf
        feeling how smooth its texture
                ants climb up the hill

Growth, Love, Nurture, Aspire, Wisdom

Infinity

Line of thought
Circle of time
Cycle of eternity

Everything is known…

once fear is faced.

Growth, Love, Nurture, Aspire, Wisdom

Within each fear
continue on,
one step at a time,
creating possibility,
moving forward.

Space and time
unite in one cause.
Life is created within
the space between
chaos and order.

Growth, Love, Nurture, Aspire, Wisdom

Build upon
what is known.
With truth and desire,
it will be shown
to you over time.

A fluttering balance…

the knowing of now.

Relate.
Release.
Fuse with the
'other'
Observe self.

You don't need to swallow a bird to know how to fly!

Perspective arises
in the viewing of
the space between and
becomes
when complete.
Time space
materializes, the
texture of oneness.

Create
an interest
in the mystery
that living 'now'
offers.

Open the space.
Blend the vibrations of
fear and joy
into one.

Concentrate on
the focus.

If I trust who I am, there is no risk, therefore no fear. Fear stops risk. Risk is the adventure, the curiosity of…

Growth, Love, Nurture, Aspire, Wisdom

Who I am,
is the
permission
you
grant me
to be.

No action is beyond what you 'see', beyond neutrality. The siZe of a miracle depends on a state of no reaction.

Growth, Love, Nurture, Aspire, Wisdom

Where is here?
The space between
everything
and nothing?
A sequence of
events, birth
to death.
Find the in between.

The only real escape is to face whatever it is and make a choice… no matter what… do not fear, as the choice you make is where you are, there is no right or wrong, just is… and down the journey more information will be obtained and another choice can be made…just a matter of time – space and allowing awakening.

Fear is mostly of one's self in the unknown moment to come – turn the perspective to excitement of what's to be – omit the fear.

What is it with this fear of fear?
All ya gotta do is look it in the face and ask "what's up?" and it goes away…

(I really don't feel it can stand the attention!)

Breathe deeply when you feel fear approaching – it hates to see you awaken!

Remember that fear and trust start within – take care of yourself.

Growth, Love, Nurture, Aspire, Wisdom

If it looks like life will pass you by – stick out your thumb and hitch a ride.

Learn to listen
to the voice from
within...
the messages
will open doors.

Growth, Love, Nurture, Aspire, Wisdom

Things aren't always as they seem.

Welcome to the pier!

Simply say.
Simply do.
Simply play.
Simply you.
Sing and dance the whole day through – play the game, love life, participate.

Growth, Love, Nurture, Aspire, Wisdom

Life is fluid.
A river running deep –
why create rocks to
interfere with
the flow?

Bring joy to each
moment and let
your fears fend
for themselves.
There are always at least
two realities to
each situation.

Growth, Love, Nurture, Aspire, Wisdom

Fear is imagined when possibility is not embraced.
Create faith in what is to be is.
Possibilities.

This life I'm in
is but a dream —
which I can create
and control that
which I foresee.

Space and time defined.
What is the meaning?
How is it felt? Movement on
a level more than felling,
where words are barely held
together as lose fitting
characters floating in
an energy field seeking
connection.

Maybe one day
I'll just say…

Why not NOW?

and let tomorrow
be like the sea.

Growth, Love, Nurture, Aspire, Wisdom

What you run from,
is where you seek.
What you find,
is your peace. Conquer
the fear, don't feel
meek. Change for you
can be so sweet.

Observation precedes wisdom.

Expand the necessity not to react conditionally. Create fluidity.

To be or
not to be,
is not the question.
To allow
being or not
is…
participate
in your life.

Growth, Love, Nurture, Aspire, Wisdom

The evening comes,
the evening sun,
all bright with me
in mind.
Come fly with me.
Go climb a tree.
Be strong. Keep going.
Be alive.
The time is near, omit
your fears. The best is
yet to come.

Being present matters.
Paying attention
without judgement.
Being open to what is there.
Sometimes participation
is just a matter of being
there completely, one
moment at a time.

Growth, Love, Nurture, Aspire, Wisdom

Break through the shell society puts you in – around you – others expectations.

Participation
appears differently
to each of us based on
our perceptions.

Freedom comes from the letting go of the thoughts, assumptions, attachments that we hold on to within the fear of loss.

When you feel fear…
pay attention to the
feeling it brings you
and remember the taste.
As I remember,
I do not fear.
In other words, fear is
no longer an unknown.

Wouldn't it be nice to
see another part
of reality?
Work through
the dreams our
choices bring.

Live dangerously?
Keep jumping in…
participate.

Growth, Love, Nurture, Aspire, Wisdom

Simply naked
to the moon.
Love and life adorned…
I swoon.

The dance –
purity of
time and space.

Our actions are based
on our perceptions,
which create
our 'world'.

Lost in the illusion that
never was,
only to awaken before
another begins...

Growth, Love, Nurture, Aspire, Wisdom

Embarrassment is wasted on the lost...

Be fulfilled now in the moment occurring, no expectations.

Growth, Love, Nurture, Aspire, Wisdom

Catch the defining moment of observation.

Mysterious,
magical,
miraculous,
marvelous
mind
maneuvers...
watch yours!

Growth, Love, Nurture, Aspire, Wisdom

Every time we pull
back, reflect, we are
opening to what's next.
No matter
if we perceive it
as going back,
we are still becoming.

Watch what you are doing... something you say Wow! to... the connecting thread, filling in the spaces.

Intensify the discomfort to intuit the knowing.

See your Wow!
Feel your Awe!

Acknowledge
the beauty you are!

Do you know the winter's crispness
as it falls across the land
the bright virgin freshness
of total being
the clean air
the shadows so fair
the lasting oneness
of ones so near
the peace of the world
with nothing to fear
but the changing of time
and the distance of mind
near yet so far from here

Spattering with joy
little flowers flying free
  their goodness to all

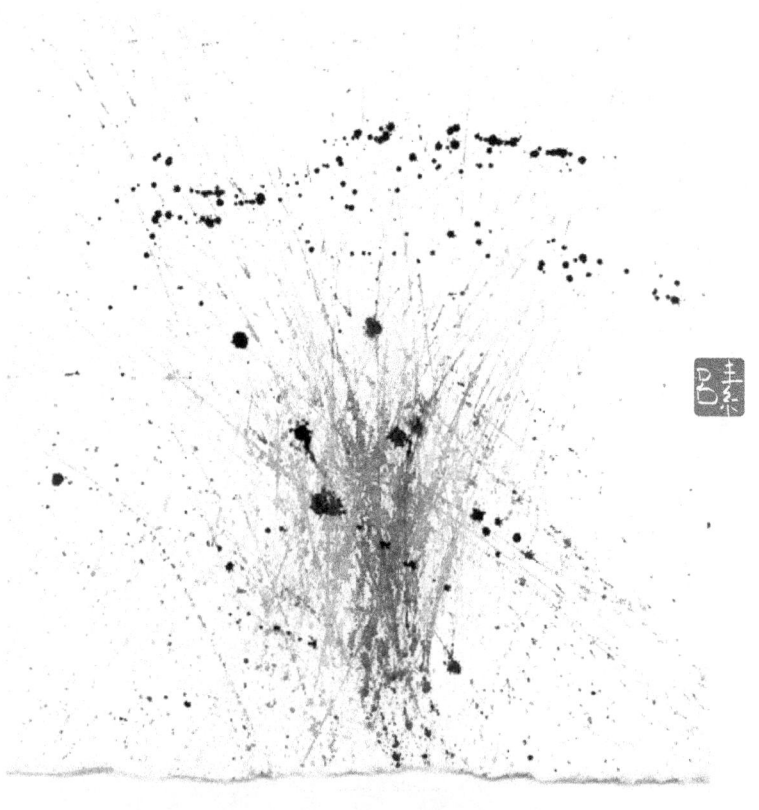

www.ingramcontent.com/pod-product-compliance
Lightning Source LLC
Chambersburg PA
CBHW051748040426
42446CB00007B/274